ROBOTS AND ROBOTICS

FIGHTING ROBOTS

RYAN NAGELHOUT

PowerKiDS press.

New York

Published in 2017 by The Rosen Publishing Group, Inc.
29 East 21st Street, New York, NY 10010

First Edition

Editor: Caitie McAneney
Book Design: Reann Nye

Photo Credits: Cover othree/https://www.flickr.com/photos/othree/14080036357; pp. 5, 6 Kurita KAKU/Gamma-Rapho/Getty Images; p. 7 http://battlebots.wikia.com/wiki/File:Diesector_SF02.jpg; p. 9 https://en.wikipedia.org/wiki/File:The_Moment_of_Victory_-_Critter_Crunch_1991.jpg; pp. 11 (lifting bot and wedge bot), 23 ROBYN BECK/AFP/Getty Images; p. 11 (spinning bot) https://commons.wikimedia.org/wiki/File:RoboCore_Robot_Combat.jpg; pp. 12, 17, 18, 19, 21 Pablo Blazquez Dominguez/Getty Images News/Getty Images; p. 13 Portland Press Herald/Getty Images; p. 15 Maureen Sullivan/Moment Mobile/Getty Images; p. 16 Charlotte Lake/Shutterstock.com; p. 25 Getty Images/Getty Images Entertainment/Getty Images; pp. 26, 27 Oakland Tribune/Tribune News Service/Getty Images; p. 30 http://battlebots.wikia.com/wiki/File:Mechadon_4.0.jpg.

Library of Congress Cataloging-in-Publication Data

Names: Nagelhout, Ryan, author.
Title: Fighting robots / Ryan Nagelhout.
Description: New York : PowerKids Press, [2017] | Series: Robots and robotics
  | Includes index.
Identifiers: LCCN 2016005683 | ISBN 9781499421637 (pbk.) | ISBN 9781499421651 (library bound) | ISBN 9781499421644 (6 pack)
Subjects: LCSH: Robots–Design and construction–Juvenile literature. |
  Robots–Control systems–Juvenile literature. | Robotics–Juvenile
  literature. | BattleBots (Television program)–Juvenile literature.
Classification: LCC TJ211 .N324 2017 | DDC 629.8/92–dc23
LC record available at http://lccn.loc.gov/2016005683

Manufactured in the United States of America

CPSIA Compliance Information: Batch #BS16PK: For Further Information contact Rosen Publishing, New York, New York at 1-800-237-9932

CONTENTS

READY TO FIGHT

Many machines are built for battle. The military uses robots in a number of different ways. Special robots can **disarm** bombs. Flying drones—machines without pilots—carry weapons and are ready to attack. However, robots aren't just the stuff of military operations or science fiction. Many people build robots, and you can, too!

Many remote-controlled, or RC, fighting robots are built to take out the competition and win the fight. Sometimes robot battles have special rules, but often your imagination is your only limit. Fighting robots are built with the motors and other basic parts all robots need. Then, robot experts can add wheels, legs, and crazy weapons to them. Creative robot technology makes robot battles exciting, fun, and full of science!

Robots are a great way to learn more about science, technology, engineering, and math, or "STEM." Building a robot requires a lot of knowledge of all four topics.

BUILT FOR BATTLE

Fighting robots come in a few different forms. Some robots are anthropomorphic, or built to **mimic** human actions and body parts. This means they walk with legs and use their arms in battle. These fights usually involve the machines trying to knock each other over.

Robots built for fighting are used only to compete against other robots. Using a fighting robot against another person is very **dangerous**.

ANTHROPOMORPHIC ROBOT

WHEELED ROBOT

Other robots are more like RC cars. They use wheels to move around and battle each other. Some wheeled robots, such as wedge robots, usually try to flip the other robot over. More **complex** machines have weapons, such as spinning arms or saws, with which to cause damage. These weapons rip off the other robot's pieces or harm the electronics that make the robot work. Because of this, fighting robots need armor made of metal or plastic for protection.

ROBOT ROOTS

In the 1970s and 1980s, some fighting robots were made at colleges, such as the Massachusetts Institute of Technology (MIT) and the California Institute of Technology (Caltech). However, it wasn't until the 1990s that robot combat really began to spread. In 1992, an **animatronics** and toy designer named Marc Thorpe tried to build an RC vacuum cleaner. Instead, he came up with an idea for fighting robots and a competition called Robot Wars. Thorpe put an ad in an RC car magazine to get interest from other RC **enthusiasts**.

Two years later, the first Robot Wars event was held in San Francisco, California. Since then, competitions have taken place all over the world. The second Robot Wars event in 1995 brought new designs and **strategies** to the competition, including the first wedge robot.

CRITTER CRUNCH

October 28, 1989, was an important day in the history of robot battles. On that day, robots first faced off in an event called Critter Crunch. It was part of MileHiCon, a gathering of sci-fi and fantasy fans in Denver, Colorado. The winner of the first Critter Crunch was a robot called Thing One. This event was just the beginning of robot fighting events and TV shows.

These engineers take part in Critter Crunch, which is considered by many to be the first robot battle of its kind.

FOLLOW THE RULES

There are many different robot competitions today, and each has a set of rules competitors must follow. For example, some competitions don't allow robots to shoot flames. Others are fine with flamethrowers attached to their robots. Just like boxing and wrestling, many robot competitions are organized by different weight classes. This means only similar-sized robots fight against each other.

Three major designs for fighting robots include the wedge, lifting robot, and spinner. The wedge robot is designed to get underneath other robots and flip them over. The lifting robot uses an arm or another mechanical device to quickly lift and flip robots over. Spinner bots do damage with metal objects that spin and hammer other robots. Each design has its advantages and disadvantages in a fight.

STAYING SAFE

Robots with weapons, such as spinning blades or big hammers, can be dangerous not only to other robots, but to people watching the battles. That's why most robot battlegrounds are enclosed in strong plastic called polycarbonate. These enclosures are see-through so fans can see all the action but still be protected from flying debris or robots. Thorpe said the first Robot Wars only had a 2-foot-high (0.6 m) railing to protect fans.

THREE BASIC FIGHTING ROBOTS

SPINNING SAW

SPINNER BOT

weapon: fast-spinning blades or bars
strength: causes damage quickly and can break other weapons
weakness: often unstable, can be flipped by wedges

LIFTING ARM

LIFTING BOT

weapon: arm or forks to flip other robots
strength: strong, can flip anything it gets underneath
weakness: arms can be broken

WEDGE

WEDGE BOT

weapon: wedge design used to flip other robots
strength: speed to avoid attacks
weakness: no weapon to cause damage

Here's a quick look at the three basic fighting robot types and how they match up against one another.

LEARNING THE GAME

The robot competitions you see on TV can get pretty violent. They're also very expensive—a robotic engineer might have to spend hundreds of dollars to repair their bot after a single match. However, not all robot contests are about robots tearing each other to pieces. Some robot competitions, especially those for high school and college students, don't include fights at all.

SUMO ROBOTS

Anyone can build a robot and compete in a robot event. You just have to find the right event for you and your robot.

Some contests have engineers move their robots through an **obstacle course**. Sumo events feature robots that need to stay on or push objects off a raised platform. Robot engineers competing in obstacle courses or sumo events have to design their robots specifically to complete these tasks. Some events have robots complete missions their engineers don't know about until the day of the competition. That means their machines need to be able to do many different things.

PIECES AND PARTS

While the designs and weapons may differ, most fighting robots are made of the same basic parts. The body of a robot is called the chassis. It holds all the different parts together in one place. Armor in the form of metal or plastic plates is added to the chassis to keep the technology inside safe from attacks. If one part of the robot's electronics is damaged or stops working properly, the entire machine might shut down.

These robots also need a battery, which gives them power. The batteries often used for small fighting robots today are similar to the ones inside a cell phone or tablet but usually a bit bigger. Today, many fighting robots are made using powerful lithium-ion batteries, which can be recharged and used many times.

You can learn a lot about robots and how they work by taking a look inside.

THREE BASIC PARTS

Whether they're used for manufacturing, underwater tasks, or fighting, robots usually have the same basic parts: sensors, actuators, and effectors. The sensors tell a robot information about its surroundings. The actuators are the motors that move the robot's parts, such as the wheels. The effectors directly interact with the robot's surroundings. Examples include grippers and claws, or weapons in the case of fighting robots. The best way to learn about robot parts and how they work together is to build one for yourself!

The battery powers the motor, and the motor **generates** the movement robots need to work. There are many different kinds of electric motors, but they all use magnetism—the attraction between certain metals—to generate the right kind of energy to make movement. A simple kind of electric motor, which is called a brushed motor, isn't very expensive and works well in simple, small robots.

Brushless motors are more expensive, but they're more reliable when controlling robots. They work quickly and generate more power, which moves larger robots or more complex systems more easily. A more complex robot often needs more than one motor to power its different parts. These robots have motors that power each side of the machine separately.

BRUSHLESS MOTOR

People who build robots use many different tools, from tiny screwdrivers to hot glue guns to tools for soldering, or melting metal together.

USING THE RADIO

Fighting robots get commands from a remote control, just like an RC car or boat. The remote control is called a transmitter because it transmits, or sends, commands to the robot. A receiver in the robot's chassis picks up these commands.

The transmitter and receiver communicate using radio technology, which sends out information through waves moving at a certain **frequency**. Both the transmitter and receiver need to be operating on the same frequency to communicate. More complicated RC transmitters use more than one channel to send information to a receiver so it can complete multiple tasks. At fighting competitions, competitors aren't allowed to jam these signals to stop other drivers from operating their robots. Everyone wants to win, but not by cheating!

The person controlling a robot doesn't need its transmitter physically connected to the robot. The transmitter uses radio waves we can't see to "talk" to the robot.

MAKING IT ALL WORK

The most important part of a robot's technology is called a speed controller. It's basically the brain of a fighting robot. It takes commands from the receiver and uses them to tell the battery how much power to send to the motors. It's important for robot engineers to make sure all of these parts work together properly. Once the robot's most important pieces are assembled and working together, the chassis and armor are added to the machine. Wheels are also added so the robot can get around. Then it's ready to fight!

Some beginning robot engineers buy fighting robot kits, which have all the parts they need to build a basic fighting robot. Others **improvise**. They can use a battery from a power tool and make the chassis out of spare parts they find in their garage.

THE BASICS

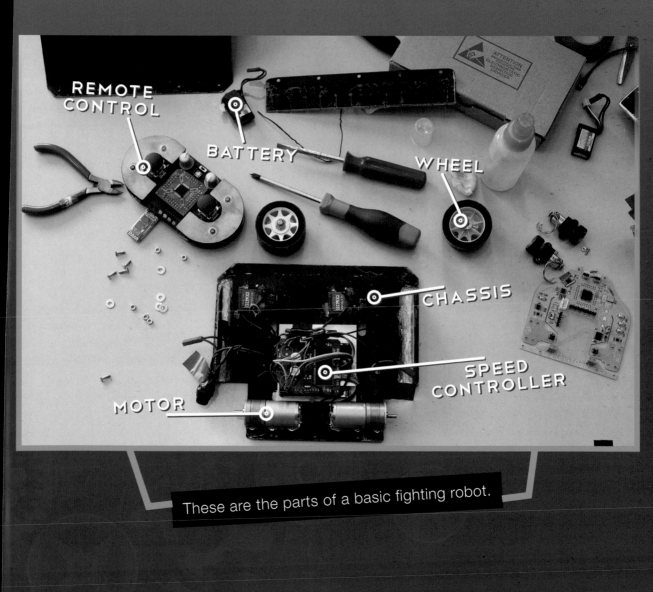

REMOTE CONTROL

BATTERY

WHEEL

CHASSIS

SPEED CONTROLLER

MOTOR

These are the parts of a basic fighting robot.

PRACTICE MAKES PERFECT

Once your robot is assembled and ready to fight, you need some driving lessons before you're really ready for battle. Many great robots have lost competitions because their creators didn't drive them the right way. Engineers must make sure their RC controllers are designed to work with the type of robot they've created. Some use wheel-shaped controllers, while others have **joysticks** to direct the robot in a certain direction.

Engineers practice driving the robot in tight spaces and learn how to use its weapons. They also figure out the best way to position the bot so it can attack while keeping its important technology safe inside the chassis. Fighting robots must be able to stop quickly. They also need to be able to drive backward so they don't get stuck and can avoid attacks!

Practicing with your robot is important because if something doesn't work right, you can fix it before the big competition. The best engineers are always improving on their designs to make the best fighting robot they can.

ROBOTS ON TV

If you'd like to build your own fighting robot and need some ideas, there are many places to watch robot combat. Lots of old matches are available to watch online, including some you wouldn't get a chance to see in person, such as competitions in Japan. There's also a chance a fighting robot competition is held near you.

BattleBots was a TV show from the early 2000s that pitted robots against each other. These robots had destructive weapons and dueled in an arena that featured saws, spinning plates, and big hammers that attacked the robots! A new *BattleBots* returned in 2015 and is still looking for new robot engineers to test their creations in front of millions of people. Do you have an idea for a great new fighting robot design?

BattleBots is a popular robot competition that airs on television in the United States. Other robot competitions take place on TV in other countries. These toys are based on robots in the original *BattleBots* show.

MEGABOTS

MegaBots is a U.S. robotics company founded in 14. Its founders are robotic engineers Gui Cavalcanti, tt Oehrlein, and Brinkley Warren. MegaBots is dedicated creating some of the largest robots on Earth. The mpany developed a giant robot named Mark II, or Mk. II, t is big enough to hold a pilot and gunner. Its gun can paintballs the size of cannonballs.

This picture shows MegaBots co-founder Gui Cavalcanti standing with the giant Mark II This robot can shoot paintballs at over

MegaBots aims to empower other robotics teams to make their own robots to compete in stadium-sized battles. In 2015, MegaBots challenged a Japanese robotics company—Suidobashi Heavy Industries—to a robot battle. MegaBot's Mark II stands 15 feet (4.6 m) tall and weighs nearly 12,000 pounds (5,443 kg). Suidobashi's robot, called Kuratas, is 13 feet (4 m) tall and weighs around 8,000 pounds (3,630 kg).

ROBOT COMBAT LEAGUE

In 2013, a special type of fighting robot did battle on TV. In *Robot Combat League*, teams of two people fought other teams, with each team controlling a humanlike robot with special equipment. One person was a robotics engineer, or "robo-tech." The other person—the "robo-jockey"—wore an exo-suit, which had sensors that measured their movement. The robot then mimicked this movement.

Each robot in *Robot Combat League* was connected to the side of the ring by a metal bar. This helped the robot stay balanced and not fall over, but it also connected the robot to its power source. The source pumped fluid into the robot very quickly. The fluid was put under pressure and moved back and forth between the power source and the robot, allowing its arms and legs to move.

THE DIFFERENT DOZEN

Mark Setrakian, an animatronics creator, competed on the show *BattleBots* in 2000. For *Robot Combat League*, he made a dozen different fighting robots that battled against one another. One robot, Scorpio, had armor made of carbon fiber, which made it lighter and a bit faster. However, carbon fiber isn't as strong as steel, which meant it would be damaged more easily. Another robot, A.X.E., had an axe head it used as a weapon. Medieval had a spike ball it used to attack other robots.

This robot built by a team from the University of Hong Kong takes part in the DARPA Robotics Challenge Trials. It's powered by hydraulic fluid, much like *Robot Combat League* robots. This robot can complete several tasks, such as opening doors, and represents how robots like this could someday perform real-world tasks.

THE FIGHTING FUTURE

From the earliest wedge bots and spinner bots to the giant Mark II, the world of fighting robots is changing every year. Robotics engineers like Setrakian and the founders of MegaBots use their imaginations to invent different ways robots can claim victory in the fighting ring.

As robot technology improves, the way robots fight each other will continue to change. New weapons, new building materials, and improved electronics will make it easier to create amazing robots. As parts get cheaper and designs improve, more people will learn how to build their own fighting robots. These budding engineers might bring new ideas and technology that will change the strategy of robot fighting competitions. What kinds of weapons would you use to make your own fighting robot?

GLOSSARY

animatronic: Of, relating to, or being a puppet or similar figure that moves by means of electronic devices.

complex: Having to do with something with many parts that work together.

dangerous: Not safe.

disarm: To make something harmless.

enthusiast: Someone passionate about a certain hobby or subject.

frequency: The number of times that something (such as a wave) is repeated in a period of time.

generate: To produce something or cause something to be produced.

improvise: To make, invent, or arrange on short notice.

joystick: A control device that allows motion in two or more directions.

mimic: To copy the way something looks, acts, or sounds.

obstacle course: A series of problems, events, or requirements that make it difficult to do something.

strategy: A plan of action to achieve a goal.

INDEX

WEBSITES

Due to the changing nature of Internet links, PowerKids Press has developed an
online list of websites related to the subject of this book. This site is updated regularly.
Please use this link to access the list: www.powerkidslinks.com/rar/fight